When God Is a Traveller

When God Is a Traveller

Arundhathi Subramaniam

HarperCollins *Publishers* India

First published in India in 2014 by
HarperCollins *Publishers* India

HarperCollins Publishers India, Cyber City, Building 10-A, Gurugram,
Haryana-122002, India
www.harpercollins.co.in

This edition published in India in 2020 by HarperCollins *Publishers*

2 4 6 8 10 9 7 5 3 1

P-ISBN: 978-93-5357-612-7
E-ISBN: 978-93-5357-613-4

Typeset in 11/15 Electra LT Regular
at SURYA, New Delhi

Printed and bound at
MicroPrints India, New Delhi

MIX
Paper
FSC FSC® C218906

This product is made of FSC®-certified and other controlled material.

HarperCollins Publishers, Macken House, 39/40 Mayor Street
Upper, Dublin 1, D01 C9W8, Ireland

Contents

WHEN GOD IS A TRAVELLER

DEEPER IN TRANSIT

Refaced

(After Imtiaz Dharker's 'Canvas')

Do I want another face?
Sometimes I do.

A face no longer disfigured
by need. A face you can turn
inside out like a sock,
never knowing the difference
between surface and interior,
soft as old wool, implacable
as peace, the fibres accustomed
to concavity,
to disuse. Accustomed
to my absence.

Black Oestrus

I could lie against you,
mouth on forehead, limbs woven
into a knot too dense
for yearning, hearing the gossamer flurry
of your breath, the wild nearness
of your heartbeat, and it still won't be

close enough.

I could swallow you,
feel the slurry of you
against palate
                    —and throat,
ravish you
with the rip, snarl
and grind of canine
and molar, taste the ancestral grape
that mothered you, your purpleness
swirling down my gullet,
and it would be a kind
of knowing,

but you still won't be
me enough.

I'm learning, love,
still learning
that there's more to desire
than this tribal shudder
in the loins.

But I'm not sure
I'm ready
for it yet—

that shock
in your daily kabuki
of shape and event.

Not yet.

Not yet
that shock
of vacancy.

Rutting

There was nothing simple about it
even then—

an eleven-year-old's hunger
for the wet perfection

of the Alhambra, the musky torsos
of football stars, ancient Egypt and Jacques Cousteau's

lurching empires of the sea, bazaars
in Mughal India, the sacred plunge

into a Cadbury's Five Star bar, Kanchenjunga, kisses bluer
than the Adriatic, honeystain of sunlight

on temple wall, a moon-lathered Parthenon, draught
of northern air in Scottish castles. The child god craving

to pop a universe
into one's mouth.

It's back again,
the lust
that is the deepest
I have known,

celebrated by paperback romances
in station bookstalls, by poets in the dungeons
of Toledo, by bards crooning foreverness
and gut-thump on FM radio
in Bombay traffic jams—

an undoing,
an unmaking,
raw
raw—

a monsoonal ferocity
of need.

And This Is about Pain Too

realizing
how much of the inside
is pure slush

the centre more wobbly
than marmalade,
more roiling
than suburban gutters in August rains.

And then later,
a long time later,
the quiet—

but for how long?

Is this what they call dum pukht,
a slow cunning Awadhi simmer
of hormone and nostalgia
and recycled need,
a deep churning
of juices
in the clay innards
of a sealed vessel,

plotting mutiny
one day
but not yet?

Leapfrog

(*'Anyone who has sufficient language nurses ambitions of writing a scripture'*—Sadhguru)

Not scripture, no,
but grant me the gasp
of bridged synapse,
the lightning alignment
of marrow, mind and blood
that allows words
to spring

from the cusp of breathsong,
from a place radiant
with birdflight and rivergreen.

Not the certainty
of stone, but grant me
the quiet logic
of rain,
of love,
of the simple calendars of my childhood
of saints aureoled by overripe lemons.

Grant me the fierce tenderness
of watching
word slither into word,
into the miraculous algae
of language,
untamed by doubt
or gravity,

words careening,
diving,
            swarming, un-
forming, wilder
than snowstorms in Antarctica, wetter
than days in Cherrapunjee,

alighting on paper, only
for a moment,
tenuous, breathing,
amphibious,
before
            leaping
to some place the voice
is still learning

to reach.

Not scripture,
but a tadpole among the stars,
unafraid to plunge
deeper
if it must—

only if it must—

into transit.

Demand

And on days like this
nothing else will do.

Nothing but that whisper
of breath against the ear.

Breath that's warm
like the sigh of palmyra trees
in Tirunelveli plantations.

Breath
that's crisp
like linen, rice-starched,
dhoop-soaked,
in a family cupboard.

Breath
to be trusted,

with a thread maybe
of something
your foremothers never knew,
or pretended not to—
the spice-mist
of hookah on winter nights

in Isfahan, or raw splatter
of Himalayan rain, or wine
baroque with the sun
of al-Andalus.

Breath
of outsider,
ancestor,
friend,

who leaves nothing more than this
signature of air
against skin,
reminding you
that there's nothing respectable
about family linen
when cupboard doors close,

reminding you
that this uncensored wilderness of greed
is simply—
or not so simply—

body.

Fit

Not a hand-me-down
not ready-to-wear,
but tailormade, hand-woven
in a loom unknown,
with pockets dark and roomy
(the left deeper than the right?),
softer than the saris my grandmother
wore as a young girl in Bauktaw,
with the faintest rumour
of dorsal fin
and wrinkles
where I need them.

How did you happen?

Lover Tongue

Perhaps I will tire
of your grammar,

find myself yearning
for the rumble of verb or the soft
flesh of pure vowel
on those mornings when I stumble
over your landscape
of unforgiving nouns.

And it's possible I will whittle away
the very ribcage
in which I once sought sanctuary,

gnaw at the unbending sinew
of ancestral norm,
sulk,
turn sophomoric,
say fuck you,
say cope up,
just to disrupt
your family symmetries
your patrician DNA.

Maybe I will simply
want something more
one day
than your bequest of semicolons—
something more final,
more silent.

But even if I turn the page
before you do,
remember I am as
dog-eared,
soiled,
puzzled,
as you are,
and as much in love.

Wearing High Heels

It was those heels
that I wore
to the Class Eight jam session.

They left red weals on my feet
as I stumbled
across the dusty JB Petit school hall.

But that night
the weedy boys
from the school next door
turned into something else—
lithe warriors,
medieval, almost epic,
dark, deccan,
bodies supple as bowstrings,
gait honed by a wisdom as old
as Patanjali
(with just a frisson
of Travolta),

their conversations fluent
as streams that burble
by motionless sages
in forest hermitages,

their senses alert
to jungle breath
and portents of sky
and recondite shifts
of womanweather.

I have grown
too tall for heels.

The boys have grown
into bankers
and soft-bellied intellectuals.

But when lights dim
and city drawing-rooms
turn vertiginous,
I see them all over again,
dark, feral,
lean-haunched,
shadowy,
shape whittled down
to what really counts—

men.

The Other Side of Tablecloths

Miss Guzder's outrage was moral:
A *girl like you—I never expected it—how could you?*

Before her, the underside
of my tablecloth—
snarling green mayhem
of equatorial rainforest,
seething beneath
an upfront view
of convent-educated daffodils.

Miss Guzder, you'd disown me still.
I unseam easily,
turn green even when determined
to stay twig-dry and rootless,
and though I always long
to be elsewhere,
I've never come unstuck
without turning
into a moist tangle
of filament, each straggling
fibre alive
to a self-inflicted
green carnage.

But I learn,
I learn,

and might just grow one day
into the seamstress you'd be proud of:

I'll suture and snip,
lazy-daisy and butcher,
love and leave,
no strings attached.

Almost Shiva

It's here again,
sweeping through my life,

ripping apart jeans, books, kurtas, income tax returns,
wiping the grin
off the Bhairavnath mask
from the Thamel street shop.

Except this time
there will be no cut-and-paste,
no frantic attempt
to get the lines right,
check the silver, count the spoons.

There's terror in the air

but as earthenware crashes
and something like flesh
blackens on the griddle,
I feel it—

the solar plexus lurch,
the shiver of guilt,

a mothwing flutter of authorship

Sharecropping

I'm wearing my mother's sari,
her blood group,
her osteo-arthritic knee.

We've voted
for different men, same governments.

In dreams she plays
among trees of rubber and betel palm
outside a home in Myanmar
while I scamper down
dark service stairways
in Bombay buildings, sharp
with the smell of urine
and kesar agarbatti
smoking out of the breast pocket
of the seventh-floor madman.

She lusted after Dev Anand,
I after Imran Khan.
On television
both still sport
headfuls of black hair.

She treads nimbly
across language.
I vowel every now and then
into mouldering inertias.

I come undone
with muzak
or a compliment.
My mother's made
of sterner stuff.

Sowing the same dream
in a different self—
the cussed logic
we both know
behind aeons
of parenting.

We talk Buddhism,
Lata Mangeshkar, plot pedicures,
late into the night,

and she watches me
ancient peasant
canny harvester,
her eyes bright
with defeat
as I grow stealthily
into her body.

Here it is then—
the treachery
of middle age,
of love.

It gets no closer than this, Mum.

Osteoporosis

You comment on the gait
of women in this country,
those above fifty,
how they roll shiplike from side to side.

Osteoporosis,
I say with the wisdom of my thirties,
a generation without HRT,

and then venture
to try the truth:
Where I live
intent doesn't translate
into action
without bottlenecks
at every joint,
every junction,
every circuit,
every street.

Sideways isn't a strategy here.
It's how we live.

Catnap

This shoebox started out
a stiff-upper-lipped quadrilateral,
Upholder of Symmetry, Proportion, Principle,
sanctuary to an upright couple
of pedigree leather moccasins.

This week
shoebox learns
to sigh
de-
    cant,
contemplate

gravity.

Old idealist softens,
grows whiskers,
paw,
drowsing chin,
slumped tail,
Arctic eye.

Form is emptiness
Emptiness is form, Shariputra.

Shoebox abdicates
shape
and Gucci worship,

secedes from
nostalgia.

Pukka sahib
learns
to purr.

A Shoebox Reminisces

I renounced shape
a long time ago,

chose
bagginess,

endless
recess-
ivity,

but there are days
when the longing
returns

and I cannot abide
the sterile cynicism
of the Anti Couples Club,
the smug peddlers
of Uni-sole Advaita.

I know it means
the saga of
two old shoes
all over again,

their grubby leather unions,
tales of childhood,
prejudice, toe jam, politics,

laces in a perpetual snarl
of knots,

footprints,

footprints.

But some days
I'm idolater enough
to want it again:
that old charade,

otherness.

Epigrams for Life after Forty

Between the doorbell
and the death knell
is the tax exemption certificate.

There are fewer capital letters
than we supposed.

Other people's stories will do.
Sticky nougatine green-and-pink stories.
Other people's stories.

Untenanting is more difficult
than unbelonging.

The body? The same alignment
of flesh, bone, the scent of soap, yesterday's
headlines, a soupçon of opera.

But there *are* choices
other than cringing vassal state
and walled medieval town.

And there is a language
of aftermath,
a language of ocean and fluttering sail,
of fishing villages malabared
by palm, and dreams laced
with arrack and moonlight.

And it can even be
enough.

Learning to Say Yes

They matter,
the minor questions—
the smell of a new wardrobe,
the eternal bus ticket
in the bag's second compartment, the leer
of the late shift security guard.

Yes, Draupadi's sari is endless

and there's no way to tame
life's wild unstoppable
bureaucracy
but this:

Fill out the form. Do it in bloody triplicate. Enrol.

Watching the Steamrollers Arrive

Language begins
to peel away from you,
the skin stretched,
no longer lubricated
by faith
in renewal.

Names have started
their dissolve. Letters smudge,
the neon is erratic, leaving half
the words in serrated eclipse.

The dots have lost
their jauntiness, the dashes their
bravado,

and the little that holds,
quivers, knows

that something behind
is being
disembowelled
by an ancient buffalo logic,
unhurried,
systematic.

The police sirens, the barking dogs, grow louder.

Flagbearers

We have you covered—
Breakdown, depression, genetics, authoritarian upbringing,
neural damage, suppression, hubris, sublimation, addiction,
Marxism, Kaliyug, planetary configurations—

Our eyes gleam
with the fervour of priests
on sacred riverbanks,
ancient domesticators
of mortality.

Even the gods inch closer
when we brand them
with our love,
our naming.

The second battle of Panipat, Samsung TV, Raja Raja
Chola, Fakhruddin Ali Ahmed, Hawkins Pressure Cooker,
J. Krishnamurti, I see I see I

And we cling,
chew,
suck,
our mouths stained
with the green salad of language,

and we pound
and chew again,
our jaws grinding the cud
of a timeless latex wisdom,

because we believe
because we must

that words tame,
words stanch,
words embalm,

words know.

Forever Connected

Geishas of the inbox,
our neural pathways paved,
synapses bridged, arteries
fibre optic, heart chakras unclogged
by the Great Express Highway,
our ducts sweetened by after-mint
and Kenny G, the peepul
between us felled
to unclutter the view,
our roads widened, drainage overhauled, stray dogs exterminated.

The lines on our route are never busy.

The arrangements are in place.
Love will follow.

Confession

('To take a homeopathic approach to the soul is to deal with the darkness in ways that are in tune with the dark.'—Thomas Moore)

It's taken time
to realize
no one survives.
Not even the ordinary.

Time to own up then
to blue throat
and gall bladder extraordinaire,

to rages pristine,
to guilt unsmeared
by mediocrity,

to separation traumas
subcontinental
and griefs that dare
to be primordial.

Time to iron out
a face corrugated
by perennial hope,

time to shrug off
the harlotry
and admit
there's nothing hygienic
about this darkness—
no potted palms,
no elevator music.

I erupt from pillars,
half-lion half-woman.

The floor space index I demand
is nothing short
of epic.

I still wait sometimes
for a flicker of revelation
but for the most part
I'm unbribable.

When I open the coffee percolator
the roof flies off.

Swimming

It's because you become
foetus at the funfair—
whirling, whooping
through a jungle
of chlorine and pickled
Mediterranean blue.

Because you realize
it's enough to be
a ferris wheel of armlegarmleg
motored by turtle brain.

Because for a moment
you could even be Him,
the Lord of Tillai,
birthing, juggling,
slaying universes
in an inspired mayhem
of limb and lust.

Because deep within your seashell heart
you hear it again,
the oceanic roar
that reminds you
that it's happening
right now.

Life is here.

WHEN GOD IS A TRAVELLER

Textile

Some days
nothing in your wardrobe satisfies,
not the heat-maddened ikats, not the secular pastels.

There's no season you can call your own.

Like others
you wait
in queues
for the drought to end

although you know everything
there is to know
about the guile and the gristle
of the heart—
its handloom desires,
                                        its spandex fantasies,
its polycot, its wear-and-tear
polytheism.

And you know
that when it happens again,

the whoosh
                of textile, versatile,
                block-printed by sun,

it will feel big enough
to put an end
to all the throbbing questions
forever.

But the winters—
they get colder each time.

And so you return
reluctantly

to digging
through the stretch
and seam and protest
of tattered muscle

deeper
into the world's oldest fabric

deeper
into the
darkening
widening
meritocracy

of the heart.

How Some Hindus Find Their Personal Gods

(for AS who wonders about ishta devtas)

It's about learning to trust
the tug
that draws you to a shadowed alcove
undisturbed
by footfall
and butter lamps,

a blue-dark coolness
where you find him
waiting patiently,
that perfect minor deity—

shy, crumbly,
oven-fresh, just a little
wry, content to play a cameo
in everyone's life but your own.

A god who looks
like he could understand
errors in translation,
blizzards on the screen,
gaps in memory,
lapses in attention,

who might even learn by rote
the fury,
the wheeze,
the Pali,
the pidgin,
the gnashing mixer-grinder,
the awkward Remington stutter
of your heart,
who could make them his own.

After that you can settle for none other.

The Way You Arrive

The way your words reach me,
phantom-walking
through all these tensile,
suspicious membranes of self.

The way you unclog
these streets and by-lanes
so I can surge
through starshine and aqueduct,
the luminous canals of a world
turned Venetian.

The way you enter
and the day's events scatter
like islands in the sea.

The way you arrive.

My Friends

They're sodden, the lot of them,
leafy, with more than a whiff
of damage,
mottled with history,
dark with grime.

God knows I've wanted them different—
less preoccupied, more jaunty,
less handle-with-care,

more airbrushed,
less prone
to impossible dreams, less perishable,

a little more willing
to soak in the sun.

They don't measure up.
They're unpunctual.
They turn suddenly tuberous.

But they matter
for their crooked smiles,
their endless distractions,
their sudden pauses—

signs that they know
how green stems twist
and thicken
as they vanish
into the dark,

making their way
through their own sticky vernacular tissues
of mud,

improvising,
blundering,
improvising—

Eight Poems for Shakuntala

1

So here you are,
just another mixed-up kid,
daughter of a sage
and celestial sex worker,
clueless
like the rest of us
about your address—
    hermitage or castle,
    earth or sky,
    here or hereafter.

What did you expect?

What could you be
but halfway,
forever interim?

What else
but goddamn
human?

2

The trick, Shakuntala,
is not to see it
as betrayal

when the sky collapses
and closes in
as four windowless walls

with a chipped Mickey Mouse magnet
on the refrigerator door

or as eviction

when the ceiling crumbles
and you walk
into a night of stars.

3

Yes, there's the grizzled sage Kanva
his clarity
    that creeps into your bones
    like warmth on a winter evening
as you watch
the milky jade
of the river Malini flow by,
serene, annotated
by cloud

and there's a home
that will live evergreen
in the folklore of tourist brochures,
    detonating
with butterflies.

But what of those nights
when all you want

is a lover's breath,

    regular,
    regular,

starlight through a diaphanous curtain,
and a respite
from too much wisdom?

4

Besides, who hasn't known Dushyanta's charms?

The smell of perspiration,
the sour sharp beginnings
of decay

that never leave a man
who's breathed the air
of courtrooms and battlefields.

A man with winedark eyes who knows
of the velvet liquors and hushed laughter
in curtained recesses.

A man whose smile is abstraction
and crowsfeet, whose gaze
is just a little shopsoiled,

whose hair, mussed
by summer winds, still crackles
with the verbal joust of distant worlds.

Who hasn't known
a man cinnamon-tongued,
stubbled
with desire

and just the right smear
    of history?

5

The same hackneyed script.
The same old cast.

Springtime
and the endless dress rehearsal—

a woman lustrous eyed,
a deer, two friends,
the lotus, the bee,
the inevitable man,
the heart's sudden anapest.

Nothing original
but the hope

of something new
between parted lips.

A kiss—
jasmine lapis moonshock.

And around the corner
with the old refrain,
this chorus,
(Sanskrit, Greek, whatever):

It's never close enough
It's never long enough
It's never enough
It's never

6

As for his amnesia,
be fair.

He recognized the moment
when he saw it—

sun   springtime   woman—

and all around
thick, warm, motiveless
green.

Can we blame him
for later erasing the snapshot
forgetting his lines
losing the plot?

We who still wander along alien shorelines
hoping one day to be stilled

by the tidal gasp
of recollection?

We whose fingers still trail the waters,
restless as seaweed,
hoping to snag
the ring in the belly of a deep river fish—

round   starlit   uncompromised?

7

What you might say to the sage:

It only makes sense
if you're looking for me too—

wild-eyed
but never despairing,

certain
I'll get through eventually

through palace and marketplace,
the smoky minarets of half-dreamed cities,

 and even if you know
 how it all ends

I need to know you're wandering the forest
repeating the lines you cannot forget—

my conversations with the wind and the deer,
my songs to the creeper,

 our endless arguments
 about beginnings and endings.

Let's hear it from you, big daddy
old man, keeper of the gates.

I need to know wise men
weep like little boys.

I need to hear your words,
    hoarse,
    parched,
    echoing

through the thickening air
and curdled fog
of this endless city—

'Come back, Shakuntala.'

8

And what you might say of the ending:

Yes, it's cosy—
family album in place,
a kid with a name
to bequeath to a country,

perhaps even a chipped magnet
on the refrigerator door.

I'm in favour of happy endings too
but not those born of bad bargains.

Next time
let there be a hermitage
in coconut green light,
    the sage and I in conversation,

two friends at the door, weaving
    garlands of fragrant dream
        through days long and riverine

and gazing at a waterfront
stunned by sun,
    my mother, on an indefinite sabbatical
        from the skies.

And let me never take for granted
this green into which I was born,

this green without ache,
this green without guile,

stippled with birdcall,
bruised with sun,

this clotted green,
this unpremeditated green.

And as wild jasmine blooms in courtrooms
and lotuses in battlefields

let warriors with winedark eyes
and hair rinsed in summer wind

gambol forever with knobble-kneed fawns
in the ancient forests of memory.

Printer's Copy

The ailing poet examines
his typescript, adds a comma, deletes
the second adjective, prunes
a line-length, cuts, sutures, enjambs,

and dies the next day.

The need to believe
there is octane enough
in a bequest of verbs

to gallop,
dive,
scoop,
abduct,
rescue

reader and writer
in the long hard ride
into the sunset.

The need to believe language
will see us through

and that old, old need
to go, typo-free, to the printer.

The City and I

(returning to Bombay after 26 November 2008)

This time we didn't circle each other,
the city and I,
    hackles raised,
    fur bristling.

This time there was space
between us
and we weren't competing.

Space enough and more

for the nose-digging librarian
and her stainless steel tiffin box,

for the Little Theatre peon
to read me endless Marathi poems
on rainy afternoons,

for the woman on the 7.10 Bhayandar slow
with green combs in her hair
to say
and say again
    He's coming to get me
    He's coming.

This time
the city surged
towards me,

        mangy,
        bruised-eyed,
        non-vaccinated,

suddenly
mine.

Or Take Mrs Salim Shaikh

Who ripples hospitably
out of her halwa-pink blouse
        and sari ('Synthetics are so practical
        to wear on trains, na?'). Who invokes
the protocol of Indian railways to ask
for your phone number even before
        the journey begins. Who unwinds
        her life story, well-oiled,
without a single split end.

        She's Hindu,
        a doctor, like her husband.
The Matron warned her
about inter-faith unions,
        but she had no doubts,
not even in '93 when others did.

Her ancestors supplied butter
        to Queen Victoria,
        His grandfather, better still,
was court dewan of Kolhapur.

'I've been lucky.'
'The gods have been good.'
'I eat and cook non-veg.'
'Many of my friends are pure brahmin,'
'My sons are circumcised.'
'My heart is pure.'
'I practise no religion,
only homeopathy.'

Over lunch she remembers
the day her mother-in-law died in her arms.
'I bathed her,
and when the body was taken away,
I told my husband
I want to be buried in the kabrastan—
it's closer to our home than the crematorium.'

Take Mrs Salim Sheikh.

Benaras

(*'Moon Light English Coaching Center; O Lebal to Standard Lebal'*—Sign on Kedar Ghat, August 2009)

Lebal One

There shall be
no collisions
as long as every cow sports
five heads
twelve legs
eight wheels
ten bicycle bells
and one moo.

Lebal Two

This pundit with the Cheddar cheese voice
has scratched his tummy
as long as that dog has dreamt
of transmigration.

Lebal Three

No board exams here.
The living are coached on dying,
the dead on rebirthing,
the priests on parody.

Manikarnika blazes
in an endless semi-final.

Lebal Four

Pizza Hut
is just one thousand years old.

Lebal Five

Each time he spits,
he unleashes a torrent
of juice,
        snot,
                stomach enzymes
and a Veda.
(Incredible India, you say.
The universe
in a globule of paan.
Profligate with
mucous and metaphysics.
Sparing only
with our semen.)

Lebal Six

Paul arrives from Kerala with brandy.
Returns with Gangajal.
(His sadhu friend and guide is ex-Naxalite.)

Lebal Seven

Maanya calls.
She asks where I am.
I am blank.
Before me, the hotel wallpaper—
a palm-fringed sea—
has turned grey with the effluents
of those that have lain here before me
contemplating death
and room service.

That evening
(Lebal Eight)
we hunt,
we thirst,
we ache,
desperate pilgrims,
fevered seekers,
for just one millimetre
of riverbank
we can call
god-forsaken.

I Speak for Those with Orange Lunch Boxes

I speak for those
with orange lunch boxes,

who play third tree
in an orchard of eight
in the annual school play,

who aren't headgirls,
games captains, class monitors,

who watch other girls fight for the seesaw
from the far wall across the sand-pit,

who remember everyone's lines
but their own,

who pelt after the school bus
their mother's breakfasts still heaving
in their gut,

who still believe
there'll be exams one day
they'll be ready for,

Those with orange lunch boxes.
I speak for them.

The Builder's Lobby

('House Builder, you have now been seen;/
You shall not build the house again.'—Gautama Buddha)

Perhaps beneath the rexine and rind
of these lives,
the odours of alien kitchens,
beliefs, groin-juices,

we share a common space

where nothing can enter,
no debentures,
no politics,
no easy fluorescence.

But it takes so long getting there
that perhaps it was never meant to be.

Housebuilders build.
Doors slam.
As we sleep
mortar hardens

its resolve.

Opacity wins.

And Here's Middle Age Again

When yesterday's scripts
strike back,
coil,
clingfilm the body.

When you spring up again,
temple builder, house builder, empire builder,

thickly spreading the spores
of that old need—

unsurprising,
tepid as beer at beach picnics—

the need
to consume,
belong, be loved.

Bones

It runs in some families
this stiffening, in the early forties,

around the knee, the need
to invest more effort

in the flexion of thumb
and maybe the more attentive

hear a wind blowing
through the card palace

of their bones—a premonition
of the crumble

of resolve and calcium
and fortitude that some call

ageing. And so they pull in their limbs
like ancient drawbridges,

watch roaring desires sputter
into gentler static

though there were always other ways to get here.

Bones—2

When the heart's sludgy tributaries
grow dry,
trust the bones.

Their dry winter wisdom
will not deceive you

for in their white chalk quarry
lies something truer

than any of the fruity varieties of love
you have known.

One day the fingers will uncurl again,
the nostrils twitch, eyes widen

and the body will return to what it's always been—
          old antenna,

tuned promiscuously
springward.

But even then,
remember,
          try to remember

the bones.

I Knew a Cat

I knew a cat
with a face like a star.

I waited for her to die
so my heart would hurt
a little less.

Now the nights are darker,
my life a little easier.

And I have returned to the tribe from which I came,
our granaries lush
with words
        and lovelessness.

Transplant

Show me a plant
that's not in search
of a pot,

that knows
whether it's meant
for orchard,
rainforest,
or jam jar,

that knows, for that matter,
if it's a creeper,
conifer,
or just an upstart crocus
too big for its boots.

You'd think it would get clearer with time.
It doesn't.

And before you know it
you have yet another potted palm
with a raging heart
of Himalayan pine.

Or just an old banyan
asking to be
                    a little less ancient,
                    a little less universal,
                    a little less absolute,
a little more bloody
bonsai.

You and I that Day in Florence

(for Gayatri)

What were we seeking that supple
radiant day when

a medieval city rearranged
its geography, kodaked itself

at several degrees to the sun?
What were we seeking,

two poets in the mood
to get lost, as a world

unravelled graciously—
bridge, cobbled street and canal, careless

effusion of silhouetted cathedral,
the endless melancholy

of the Arno, and the shimmer
of trade on the Ponte Vecchio?

We asked for coffee with a frisson
of alcohol. We asked for just one man

(and there were many)
who looked like Al Pacino.

But that endless autumn day in the year 2000
it was enough to participate

in this great elsewhere, to be included
in a page from the library books

of our childhood, crisp, transfigured
by burnt dreamlight. It was enough (remember?)

to be part of the picture.

Where the Script Ends

His shirt is tangerine,
the sky Delft,
the sunshine daffodils.

Even jealousy gleams brighter here
than broccoli
                    stir fried.

In this daytime land
the canals speak
an unambiguous tongue.

We look over our shoulder
for a hint
of Venice.

All languages are honest here,
just none honest enough.

At home he speaks a dialect
he's never written in—
not even when his mother died.

And I know what it is to live
in a place where the mind's ink
has many tributaries, fermented enough
to make all songs
seem just a little
untrue.

It doesn't matter
whether he reads my lips
or I his mandarin fine print

because it still makes sense,
the old dream—

woman and man
under a night sky

and for a moment between them,
a single moon.

The Dark Night of Kitchen Sinks

I know you of course—

your familiar swamp of grease
and indignity,

knives and spoons scattered
like mutilated limbs

across a battlefield
of gravy-streaked plates
and wounded china.

After the civilities
of supper, I've heard the Huns
of cutlery (who hasn't?) unleashing
their true selves—
jostle,
        raid, ravish,
slump.

And I recognize you,
just another kitchen sink
dreaming
of foam and equanimity.

Another lifetime and we'll get there, I promise—
creamy
lavender-scented
        pH-balanced.

For now, your dreams smell of detergent
and mine of love.

It could be enough.

Jogger's Park

This, at a pinch, could be community—

with every step ahead
we grow lighter
in the faith
that there will be reprieve
from the swaddling grammar
of the flesh,
from the 70s' sitcoms
of the mind.

This is as collective as desire ever gets.

From the shape-shifting lard
of history,
from worlds we never made,
from bodies we don't understand,
from words, hi cal and greasy,

from muscle losing the cornflour starch
of certainty,

we emerge,
flushed innocents,
ready
to be fished out
of ourselves.

Hierarchies of Crisis

(for Jerry)

You remember those evenings
when they said the catastrophe was out there
and we listened,

pretending we needed them to teach us
its code,

pretending we knew nothing
of its dyslexia,

its empty gaze,
its shuttered madness,

the rabid tangle
of pain under the sheets,

the texture of rubble
and the bombing that never stops?

You remember those evenings
when we accepted

that this was the way it was—
our art
was elitist,
our silence
defeatist,
our minds
scrambled,
our ideas
poached,
our suffering
thrice-removed?

Dream on, they said,
that someone gives a damn
about your private music

of sighs and glottal stops,
and we thought they were right.

We thought everyone else was always too busy
fighting long distance

for the right to breathe—in Sudan,
or Jharkhand or some bathroom in Malibu—

and we were alone
on night rides that never ended.

Irony helped
and billboards.

We had one that said
Caution.
Wet paint.
Shows no sign of drying.

Another went
The world's oldest masquerade—
Language
pretending it's shared.

We knew even then it wasn't true.
Paint dries.
Rides end.
Language leaks.

The billboards, they remain.

Living with Earthquakes

When He comes
Out of the blue
A meteorite
Shattering your home
Be sure
God is visiting you.

—Tukaram
(Translated by Dilip Chitre)

You thought you asked for peace,

thought there would be time
to contemplate

a modular kitchen,
a beloved's eyes over a glass of rosé,
        a world spinning gracefully out of orbit
        outside a soundproof window.

You never expected this architecture

of thinning girder,
    collapsing
        beam,

this glass elevator

    plummeting

past picnicking families,
Pomeranians in suburban gardens,
sturdy investment bankers,

vaporizing faces,
names losing their voltage—

this scaffold of air.

You didn't smell the danger,
never picked up the clues.

Outside, the view blurs—
sun-baked pyramid to pagoda,
river valley to moraine—

and the devourer of form,
once a genteel termite,
now at your jugular, foaming,
inflamed
by bloodlust, almost
familiar.

So this is what you summoned
those nights
when the universe seemed not to listen,

not peace,

but this carnival
                    of unmooring,

this catamaran love.

Quick-fix Memos for Difficult Days

1

Clear
clothes, pillows, books, letters
of the germs of need—
the need to have things mean
more than they do.

Claim verticality.

2

Trust only the words that begin
their patter
in the rain-shadow valley
of the mind.

3

Some nights
you've seen
enough earth
and sky
for one lifetime

but know you still have unfinished business with both.

4

So here again,
that old cliché, pain,
and its endless syntax
of gurgle and clot.

But better swamp—
always better swamp—
than scrubland.

5

Settling is bondage.
Wandering, vagabondage.
(Someone said that before?)

(Citizenship is bondage.
Dual citizenship, James Bondage.
That's a first!)

6

Once you know
what it's like
to be chieftain,
serf, concubine
and prop,
what's left?

You choose story
or you choose curtains

story
curtains

story
curtains

until you're done with both.

7

Once you've seen grain
you don't settle for acrylic emulsion.

8

Stretch
until you reach
the edge,

then consider a pause.
(It's usually worth it.)

9

When they vanish,
leave the door open.

Gingerbread boys
run away but return eventually
to their bakers.

Bhakti (with some adulteration)

If you were coffee
I wouldn't live my life
in a coffee shop
getting my fix
on your beans.
Public lust isn't my thing.

Allow me
some deluxe delusions.

Allow me to uncork you
in the middle
of days that rattle like Coke cans,
blow through alleys like old Sunday tabloids,
so I can steal a whiff,
a whiff, no more,
of your crazy liquor.

Decant into my hipflask. Settle down in my pocket. Stay illicit.

Shoe Zen

It takes much tongue-wagging
to fashion speech
out of the daily rituals
of occupancy
and desertion,

out of memories
of factory beginnings
and portents
of junkyard ends
and dreams
of royal mojri-hood.

Then one day
a language is born
full-blown, runic,
with the faintest aftertaste of acid
in its bite.

Until Shoe discovers
it has a double
who speaks it too.

Then Shoe learns to shut up,
allows discovery to turn
into common wisdom.

Grows rubber-soled,
learns to walk alone.

Question: What is the sound of one shoe walking?

Border

This morning at the
window, white crane on green palm
taking flight into

a greater greenness.
A rock-face sky fractured by
possibility.

Tribal thump
of poem-heart. Frantic pulse
of phloem. A bird

            unpinioned from starched
metrics. And I from gridlocked
opinion. Between

us, just this thinnest
skin of disbelief, almost
vanquishable. Al-

most vanquishable.
Almost.

Six About Love Stories

While I was waiting eagerly for him
saying to myself,

'If I see you anywhere
I'll gather you
and eat you up,'

he beat me to it
and devoured me entire…
—Nammalvar
(Translated by A.K. Ramanujan)

1

When the hunter's arrow pierces
the union
of birds
it is the beginning
of the story—

an anguish of feathers
the memory of nests
a prosody of loss.

And yet for a while,
we've been there, you and I,
amateurs
unsinged by narrative.

We wore another grammar.
It flashed like chain mail
in the sun.

Even the gods eavesdropped on our whispers.

Between us
we had seventeen words
to describe the moon.

2

A story must have bone,
a long dreaming Euphrates
of a tail,
      twitching, incised
            by a shiver of illogic.

Moon enough
to allow one lone frog
to drip endless reverie
on a winter night.

Nerve. Plenty
of nerve.

Some awaken.
Some sedate.
I need both
in different
(homeopathic)
doses.

Be my story.

3

Some stories have holes.
Some don't join the dots.
Sometimes the only way from middle to end
    is the leap.

Some are long, frayed,
open-mawed,
sticky with promise,
    lotus-petalled,
        frog-tongued,
sanctuary for flies drunk
on green noonflight.

Some stories devour other stories.

I recognize you.

4

I'd like a pond
fermented by vineyards of sun

where dragonflies gaze
at mountains ribboned
by minnow and drunken cloud

where the light is ice crystals
and sweet lime.

Let's pause here

and forget
that this hushed poise of leaf
conceals another legend—
incendiary like our own.

For a while, love,
let's pretend
there's something like a still pond.

5

I'd build a story complete
with suspect and alibi
from my handbag's deepest compartment
for you

squeezing every drop of memory
out of the shell from the Lake of Galilee,
a Portuguese banker's visiting card,
a safety pin,
bindis from Matunga Market,

if it could get me closer.

I'd suck you to the marrow
like a drumstick
and throw away the sapless corpse

if it could get me closer

I'll fax, photocopy,
read us in translation forever, if I must.

But as the world around us shrieks
and rages and babbles in tongues,
promise me,

promise me there's an original.

6

Much as I dislike
locks, bolts, keys, security checks
I do like frames.

And to hear our murmurs
I see the need for enclosure.

Let them stay,
the beams, lintels, columns.
And I'm not immune
to the charms sometimes
of a good old-fashioned doorway
where you stoop a little to enter
from dazzling light
to dark invitation.

                    What the hell,
add a password, if you must.

Outside the night winds howl,
      democratically intimate.

Let's defer that story.

When God Is a Traveller

(wondering about Kartikeya/ Muruga/ Subramania,
my namesake)

Trust the god
back from his travels,

his voice wholegrain
    (and chamomile),
his wisdom neem,
    his peacock, sweaty-plumed,
    drowsing in the shadows.

Trust him
who sits wordless on park benches
listening to the cries of children
fading into the dusk,
his gaze emptied of vagrancy,
his heart of ownership.

Trust him
who has seen enough—
revolutions, promises, the desperate light
of shopping malls, hospital rooms,
manifestos, theologies, the iron taste
of blood, the great craters in the middle
            of love.

Trust him
who no longer begrudges
his brother his prize,
his parents their partisanship.

Trust him
whose race is run,
whose journey remains,

who stands fluid-stemmed
knowing he is the tree
that bears fruit, festive
with sun.

Trust him
who recognizes you—
auspicious, abundant, battle-scarred,
                alive—
and knows from where you come.

Trust the god
ready to circle the world all over again
this time for no reason at all
other than to see it
through your eyes.

Poems Matter

It was snobbery perhaps
(or habit)

    to want
    perforation,

to choose cotton, for instance,
with its coarse asymmetries,
over polyester
or unctuous rayon.

But this, I suppose,
is what we were looking for all along—
this weave
that dares to embrace

                air,

this hush of linen, these frayed edges,
these places where thought
runs
              threadbare,
where colours bleed into
something vastly blue
like sky,

these tatters
at peace almost
with the great outrage
of not being around.

It's taken a long time
to understand
poems matter
because they have holes.

Acknowledgements

The poems of *Deeper in Transit* are from Arundhathi Subramaniam's collection *Where I Live: New and Selected Poems* (2009), published in the UK by Bloodaxe Books.

The poems of *When God Is a Traveller* are previously uncollected, and acknowledgements are due to the editors of the following publications in which some of these poems, at times in different versions, first appeared: *The Literary Review Indian Poetry* (New Jersey: Fairleigh Dickinson University), *The Yellow Nib Contemporary English Poetry by Indians* (Belfast: Queens University), *World Literature Today: Writing from Modern India* (Norman: University of Oklahoma), *The HarperCollins Book of English Poetry by Indians, The Brown Critique, The Missing Slate, English* (KEYwording Series, Living Archive Project, Arsenal—Institute for Film and Video Art, Berlin), *IQ—Indian Quarterly* and *Muse India*.

'Why language? They
ask, why not medicine
or magic? Why not
something more useful?'
(Kala Krishnan Ramesh)

The editors at HarperCollins believe that poetry is medicine, magic and more. Committed to publishing the most exciting contemporary poetry from India and the subcontinent, we wanted to celebrate ten of our favourite books by publishing them as special keepsake editions under the 'Poetry 10' series. From sci-fi verse to modern bhakti poetry, long narrative sequences about birth and identity to brief sonnets, each book will speak to lovers (and haters) of poetry with wit, wisdom, clarity and abandon.

3 Sections by Vijay Seshadri
All One's Blue by Kazim Ali
Bearings by Karthika Naïr
Countries of the Body by Tishani Doshi
He Is Honey, Salt and the Most Perfect Grammar by Kala Krishnan Ramesh
Life & Times of Mr S by Vivek Narayanan
Malabar Mind by Anita Nair
Space Gulliver: Chronicles of an Alien by Sampurna Chattarji
Triage: Casualties of Love and Sex by Margaret Mascarenhas
When God Is a Traveller by Arundhathi Subramaniam

Arundhathi Subramaniam's poems explore ambivalences – the desire for adventure and anchorage, expansion and containment, vulnerability and strength, freedom and belonging, withdrawal and engagement, language as exciting resource and as desperate refuge. These are poems of wonder and precarious elation, and all the roadblocks and rewards on the long dangerous route to recovering what it is to be alive and human. Winner of the inaugural Khushwant Singh Poetry Prize and shortlisted for the 2014 T.S. Eliot Prize, *When God Is a Traveller* is a remarkable book of poetry.